The Calm Before

Pat Grieco

Grieco

Other Books by Pat Grieco

The Art of Nauga Farming

Compulsion

Rhetoric

The Book of Light

Keep the Dance

The Calm Before

First Print Edition

Print edition produced in the United States of America

Cover photo: Pat Grieco

Print ISBN: 978-0-9997944-4-9

Pen and Lute
www.penandlute.com

The final approval for this literary material is granted by the author.

Library of Congress Control Number: 2019919536

Distributed Publication
Lexington, KY
Middletown, DE
San Bernardino. CA

DEDICATION

For those who see what is to come and persevere

The Calm Before

We are defined by the difference
between what we want to do
and what we actually do.

The gap between them is immeasurable
and the persons separated by that gap
are unrecognizable to each other.

The Calm Before

Pat Grieco

The Calm Before

CONTENTS

The Calm Before 1

Five Cards..2

Cat and Mouse..3

Darkness and Light..4

A matter of personhood..8

Washed clean..14

Just one man 17

A Pebble 20

False Prophets..26

The power of prayer 30

For the fallen ones 32

Empty seat 34

Eileen..36

The old man said 39

Poison bearing fruit 41

No other..51

As I watched you go..57

That tattered, battered cloth..60

Glory..66

Still life 70

Gold Star..74

Onward to Thermopylae..77

Impressions of a Winter's Day 82

Grieco

Among the Stones 85

Alone 87

Stories 90

Gatekeeper 92

Half faced man 95

The Calm Before

This is a favorite part of the day,
the calm before the storm,
when all things are still possible,
before our fates become entwined
with the violence of the storm
and we must fight
against the currents of the gale
to survive,
to see the dawning of the next.

The thunder
breaks upon the sun baked hills,
and clouds,
dark and boiling
with the anger of the storm,
begin their march
upon the peacefulness below.

Yet all is still possible.
The storm may pass us by.
It may spend itself upon the hills.
We may flee to safety
where the sun shines still.
We may stay
and brave the onslaught
as it spends its fury
to release its woe.

All,
all is yet to come
in this calm before the storm,
but our choices
and the storm
shall shape what follows.

The Calm Before

Five Cards

It all begins with the cards you hold.
Five cards
and the one who holds them,
inseparable while they are in play.
Nothing else exists.

With these cards the questions come.
Do I play the hand I have?
Is it good enough?
Are these the cards I want?
What do I risk if I throw these down?
What might I get if I take new ones?
Does the risk outweigh the looked-for gain?

Each ponders these
in the moment of decision
gazing at the cards held.
Hold, draw, or fold?
Up the ante or see
to test what chance has dealt?

The whole world shifts
at that moment of decision.
Possibilities cease
and new ones appear
all because this card was kept
and another discarded.

Win or lose,
it all depends on how the hand is viewed
and the choices made.

It all begins with the cards you hold
and how you choose to play them.

Cat and Mouse

"Come." said the Field Mouse, "We must flee.
Snake is a hidin' behind that tree.
He's sure to get us don't you see?"
But the Cat just said, "Yum Yum".
But the Cat just said, "Yum Yum".

"Please," said the Field Mouse, "run with me.
Snake is a slidin' there behind thee.
He'll eat you first and then he'll eat me."
But the Cat just said, "Yum Yum".
But the Cat just said, "Yum Yum".

"Cat," said the Field Mouse on his knees.
"Snake is behind you, don't you see?
His dinner's made while me you tease."
But the Cat just said, "Yum Yum."
But the Cat just said, "Yum Yum."

"Mouse," said the Cat alight with glee.
"I'd foolish be if I did flee.
When I catch you my dinner you'll be."
But the Snake just said, "Yum, Yum".
But the Snake just said, "Yum, Yum".

Said Cat to the Field Mouse, "Please help me.
Snake is a got me, his dinner I'll be
Unless you stay and pull me free."
But the Mousee he did run.
And the Snake just said, "Yum, Yum".

The Calm Before

Darkness and Light

There is a line they say
between darkness and light,
between night and day,
between our beasts
and our better natures.

It is distinct.
It is sharp.
It is clear,
that dim and shadowed line,
where all the in-betweens reside,
where the world is gray and fuzzy,
where nothing is completely as it seems.

On this side
darkness,
solid and complete,
ripe with horrors
too terrible to contemplate
and riches
too vast to ignore.

On that side
light,
bright with hope
and purpose,
clear,
with faith
the one sustaining virtue
bringing vision
to this transparent world
of clarity,
justice,
and right.

Grieco

No one lives there,
in the darkness
or in the light,
and those who think they do
are fools or worse
posturing for effect,
claiming the mantle of either
for their own purposes.

Darkness wrapped in light
is wielded like a sword
to cut away dissent,
to erase opposition,
to silence those beyond
the line so sharply drawn.

Offering security,
it is used to control those
more malleable,
more trusting,
more attuned to the essence
claimed,
but not earned.

And those folk,
believing they reside in light,
confuse belief
with righteousness,
faith
with correctness,
and clarity of view
with truth.

With the face of innocents,
much is done in the name of purity,
many dark and dreadful things
occur under the guise

The Calm Before

of correcting wrong,
of preserving sanctity,
with no thought
that these things
be less than justified,
that faith,
unquestioned,
could be anything
but a healing agent
for the body of believers
and for those
not numbered among them.

Darkness and Light.
Alike in their absolutes.
Alike in their completeness.
Alike in their barren disregard
for the line between,
for the shadows where life occurs,
where change and choice,
right and wrong,
faith and non-belief
merge together in a substance
accepted as real
and seen for other than it is.

There is a line they say
between darkness and light,
between night and day,
between our beasts
and our better natures.

But it is untrue,
a lie if you will
to protect both weak and strong
in their existence.

Grieco

For what you are,
what you see,
what degree of darkness or light
is embraced or simply ignored
depends on what you choose.

Choose and make a world
bathed in sweetness or despair
but regardless of the chosen world,
the pain or joy contained within,
it,
and all else
exist within the line,
between the absolutes.

It is only there
that one may find our true nature.
It is only there
that we live,
beings neither dark nor light,
defining our lives and ourselves
within that line
where all,
all,
is shadow.

The Calm Before

A matter of personhood

The learnéd ones all gathered round
dressed in their learnéd robes
and studied learnéd writings
while stroking learnéd lobes.

They peered through learnéd volumes,
thick with learnéd thoughts,
making learnéd judgments
as they gathered round to talk.

They seemed so full of wisdom,
though it turned out all along
that in the simplest judgment
they were completely wrong.

Some thought that it was hubris.
Some thought it merely pride
that led them to their error,
that led them to decide

that a business corporation
was the same as you and me
with rights and voice and liberties
with yearnings to be free

to spend their mounds of money
to support those candidates
most likely to support their views
while deciding all our fates.

The learnéd ones consulted
behind their chamber doors
upon the grant of personhood
deciding five to four.

Strange to think that learnéd ones
would make a judgment so
to grant a business personhood
delivered quite a blow

to those of us who live and breathe
whose blood is bright and red
and not a blend of pulp and ink
or brick and stone instead.

For a business has no standing
in the mountains or the sand
where actual folks die fighting
in the strife of foreign lands

and business suffers from no pain
or body's many ills
it merely suffers from the lack
of money in its till.

A business cannot skin its knee
or cry in mother's arms
although we all agree I'm sure
a business can do harm

through its carelessness or greed
in search of corporate goals
while we the people are the ones
for whom the bell must toll.

A business does not go to jail.
It does not live or die.
It cannot now appreciate
the beauty of the sky.

The Calm Before

A business has no arms or legs
although its reach is long.
A business cannot write a play
or burst into a song.

A business does not fall in love.
Its heart's not split in twain
at thought that dear belovéd's face
will not be seen again.

A business cares not who it hurts
though there it shares a trait
with folk who seek to gain their way
through cheating, lies, and hate.

And like some folk a business kills
by practice less than fair
when shortcuts and substandard stuff
becomes the freight to bear

for ever higher profits
regardless of the cost
in terms of human suffering
as casually they toss

away the very standards
meant to guard humanity
or something somewhat simpler
like our food chain or the bees.

And yet the learnéd ones' decree
awarded personhood
upon the faceless businesses
that hold not public good

more important than their profits
or their stock bound dividends
and so they spend their money
on the ones they hope to send

off to higher office
bought and paid for is their vote
for if it's not then businesses
will next time surely note

and pay for other people
who will surely vote their way
denying even science
if it dares to have its say

with inconvenient secrets,
with inconvenient truths
unless its might be neutered
within the voting booth

and after that be silenced
as a nuisance or at best
as just some frightened ramblings
or an educated guess.

Yes, a business has no standing
as we count humanity.
A business surely can not vote
from sea to shining sea

and thus it should not have a voice
in how these things are done,
in how elections come about,
in how they're lost or won.

The Calm Before

For if profit then becomes the key
to who may win or lose
with candidates all the same
no matter who we choose

then soon enough we'll have no vote
as business comes to rule
with those we send to Congress
nothing more than corporate tools

to shape the legislation,
to change the rules and law
in the quest for greater profits
to fill the corporate maw

while stripping 'way our freedoms,
our liberties and rights
to sue the corporate giants
with chance of equal fight

when wrongs have been committed
and earth and sky and sea
no longer fit to live within
or use by you and me.

They'll be no drumbeats sounding.
They'll be no trumpet's call
when corporate voice is all that's heard
within Congressional halls.

But learnéd ones have spoken
on what personhood should be
and with a stroke of learnéd pen
destroyed democracy

or at least have made it futile
for our voice no longer counts
as the damage to the climate
and our liberties now mount.

Soon we'll pay the piper
for decisions made and then
the finger must be pointed
at those five most learnéd men

when in simple grant of personhood
would never have assumed
that their reasoned, learnéd action
would send us to our doom.

The Calm Before

Washed clean

They sold their souls at daybreak
then swiftly knelt to pray
to ask God for forgiveness
for all they'd do that day.

For a felony was not a crime
and truth was not the truth,
really just illusions
from their guiltless, blameless youth

and mothers and their children
would be turned away in fear
and vilified as evil,
scorned without a tear

and faith would be a weapon
instead of sacred shield,
used to bludgeon any foes
and force them all to yield.

For power was the only goal,
kept at any cost,
with never any waking thought
for all that they had lost.

Deep there in the darkness,
where they knelt in prayer,
there was no room for Others,
there was no thought to share

the most abundant riches
offered by this land
but even as they held them close
they slipped away like sand.

Grieco

They said they served the many
in fact they served the few
and as they knelt there in the dark,
they knew, they knew

that every promise made
was only for the rich
and not for all the common folk
believing every pitch.

"Believe we are your only hope,
that fear and hate are good,
that only we can keep you safe
in your neighborhoods.

Believe that we will help you.
Believe that lies are true.
Believe the Others swarm like hordes
though their numbers be but few.

And when you act on what we say,
you will be in the right.
Just ignore your conscience,
so you can sleep at night."

The common folk then bowed their heads
and prayed to wash away
what in the past they'd not accept
but found now every day

accepted here as normal
by their neighbors and their kin
and by religious leaders
who pray to God and then

forget what they have witnessed,
ignore what they have seen,

The Calm Before

for after all they've knelt and prayed
and so their hands are clean,

washed with the blood of innocents,
washed clean to join with those
who knelt to pray at daybreak
and in darkness sold their souls.

Just one man

He was just one man,
flawed and imperfect
in many ways
as are we all.

He did not have all the answers
but he knew that they existed
if people of good will
and conscience
worked together,
hand-in-hand,
to find them.

He spoke to our better selves
but recognized the danger
and the ugliness that often exists
within our lesser.

He realized that the best of intentions
must be matched with action
to ensure that the intent
is not lost somewhere along the way.

He knew that change
does not come without sacrifice
but that change must come
if we are to better ourselves
as individuals,
as a people,
and as a nation.

Yes,
he was a flawed and imperfect man
but he dreamt of a world

The Calm Before

where equality and the rights of all
would be a given
and not a privilege
of those more favored.

He spoke
because others could not.

He marched
even when the road was long
and the way uncertain.

He did not seek the spotlight
nor did he avoid it when it came.
Rather he saw the all-consuming light
as a cure for a blindness
most did not know they had.

He did what he could
to improve the lot of others
and gave his everything
so that others might not have to.

He was just one man
but his life showed
that all are capable
of extraordinary things
if their belief is strong
and the cause is just.

Let us not see him
for more than he was
but what he was, was enough
to inspire those who follow,
who believe the future
must be better than today,
who look for justice

in the here and now
as well as in the hereafter
and work with all their might
to make it so.

The future is not built
by the efforts of just one individual
but it sometimes takes just one
to show the rest the way to go,
the path to follow,
and the end that must be sought.

He was just one man...

The Calm Before

A Pebble

He was the best-looking dead man
I'd ever seen.
Sunday suit,
gentle smile,
hands resting lightly
on his still stomach
as he lay there
within his padded box.

It was not at all
as I had seen him last,
sitting on the sidewalk
in the cold October rain,
coughing up a lung
with deep, throaty sounds
wet with phlegm
and thick from cigarettes and hooch.

He'd sat there,
huddled under plastic poncho,
wearing a thick, green, hooded sweatshirt
he'd found somewhere,
now stained and dirty
from months of wear,
with trousers
of some indistinguishable shade of gray,
and boots
that only matched
in the degree of wear shown by each.

"Move out of the rain.
You'll catch your death."
"I'm dead already." he'd replied.
"Or as good as.

TB."

He'd coughed again.
This time spewing gobs
of red tinged phlegm
into the torn and ratty T-shirt
he'd use to cover his mouth.

When he could breathe again
he continued,
gesturing with the rain-soaked cloth.
"Yea, I'm dead already
but I'd rather be dead out here,
in the open being washed clean
than in some dark, flea bitten shelter.
A man can face himself outside
and know himself for what he is."

He nodded to himself,
rain dripping from the poncho's hood.
"You can think.
You can see it all right here,
and here,
and here." he said
pointing to his head,
and chest,
and ragged cloth
clutched in his left hand.

"I'm dead Ben.
And I'm not afraid of that.
I was always more afraid of life
than of death.
Of being hurt,
hurt in every way a man can be,
that I shut myself away
in books,

The Calm Before

in religion,
in booze,
'til I wasn't a man at all,
just some shadow in the sun,
a spot upon a bright world
of motion, noise, and realness.

Shoot.
I was a Doctor."
He laughed, short and quick.
"A Doctor for Christ sake.
I knew what I was doing.
Knew I was out of touch
with everything that mattered
but I was scared,
too scared I'd fail,
too scared I'd disappoint others,
too scared I'd succeed
and be expected to be more than I was,
of what I knew myself to be...
a sham,
an imposter,
a man in a white coat
pretending to heal others
when he couldn't even heal himself."

He spasmed for a moment
as he fought for control
then cleared his throat
and spat a gob of green upon the ground
where the rain worked at it awhile.

"I'm dead Ben,
but I'm more alive now
than when I had a job,
a wife,
a life,

and all the little things that came with it."

He coughed,
more violently this time,
body wracked with the effort
and when he stopped,
he leaned back against the building wall,
eyes closed as the rain washed down his face,
so many tears for the wasted years.

"Ben." he said weakly.
"It was only after I ended here,
after I died,
that I understood what living was.

All I ever had to do was be,
just be,
like a pebble in a stream,
immersed in the water,
moved by it,
but always a pebble,
never a stone,
never the water.

I could have been me,
not someone else's version,
not someone else's expectation,
not even my own...
simply a pebble."

He opened his eyes briefly
to look tiredly, searchingly at me.
"Do you understand Ben?
Do you know what I'm telling you?"

I sighed and shook my head.
"No Tom.

The Calm Before

I don't.
All I know is that it's cold and wet
and I need to get you inside
and looked after."

Tom laughed,
as if genuinely amused.
"Too late Ben." he'd said.
"Too late for that."

He seemed to settle into himself,
sinking beneath the surface.
He opened one eye,
took a ragged breath and softly said,
"You'll see Ben.
You'll understand,
when it's time."

He smiled then,
almost like the one he wore now,
warm and dry in his box,
whispered almost too low
for me to hear,
"A pebble...",
and was gone.

"I'll bury you tomorrow Tom,
but I don't understand,
won't pretend that I do.
I don't even agree
with what you said.

Goddamn it Tom!
We're not pebbles.
We're not some helpless piece of stone
mired in some rushing stream.
We can act.

Grieco

We can choose.
We can even change the stream
if we're bold enough
and smart enough
and strong enough.

Tom.
You were my brother.
You should have known.
You should have been better,
should have fought longer,
shouldn't have died
on some godforsaken sidewalk,
a stranger to all who passed
except for me,
who found you too late
after you were washed clean,
after you had surrendered yourself,
after you had become
a pebble."

He was the best-looking dead man
I had ever seen...

The Calm Before

False Prophets

FEAR!
The end is near
for *they* **are among you.**

You do not know who *they* are.
You cannot tell *them* from your friends
for *they* may be your friends,
your neighbors,
your children,
perhaps even your spouse.

They think differently than we do.
They believe differently than we do.
And *they* are a threat
to *everything* we are.

TRUST us
for we will find *them* for you.
We will root *them* out
in all *their* evil.
We will kill *them* all
and keep you safe
and secure.

When we catch *them*,
and we will,
we will use torture
to get *them* to tell us
what *they* think
we want to hear.

And if *they* evade our search

we will destroy *their* homes,
kill *their* families,
their friends,
and other innocents
for after all
they have done much worse
and this will serve
as a deterrent
and keep you safe
in the future.

You may rest easy with us in charge
for we know who *they* are.
We see *them* there
as *they* whisper in dark corners
and plot against us.

Elect us
and all will be well.

Let us lead
and we will show you the way.

Give us power
and we will use it
but only against *them*,
never you,
never those
who support us in this quest.

Of course we must take steps
to root *them* out.
We must see everything *they* do,
watch every keystroke,
listen to every word,
be mindful of each step,

The Calm Before

each journey,
each conversation.

And if we must do that
to you as well,
you will understand
that we *must*
to separate *them*
from you,
to keep you safe
and weed out
all the malcontents
and those who would disrupt
the proper order of things.

You will lose *some* liberties
but surely you won't mind.
It is after all in your best interests
that we know everything you do,
everything you say,
perhaps even what you think.
For then we can find *them*
more easily
and prevent atrocities
before they can occur.

It might be necessary
to restrict the press
for they report
all sorts of false things
and might just let *them*
know what we are doing
and we must be sure after all
that only the truth gets out.

Access to internet

and other means of communication
may need to be curtailed
to ensure that *they* have no access,
that *their* plans
can be discovered
and *they* can be destroyed.

This *might* affect you some
but it will only be an inconvenience
far outweighed
by the benefits that will ensure.

Trust us.
We would never use this
against you,
our friends,
our fellow country folk.

Vote for us
and we will keep you safe
until you become *them*,
until you disagree with us,
with our policies,
with our grip
on everything you do,
read,
hear,
and think.

FEAR!
The end is near
for *they* are among you.

The Calm Before

The power of prayer

They gave their thoughts and prayers
when they heard about the violence,
the killings and the mayhem,
and shook their heads in disbelief
that anyone could do such a thing.

They prayed when they saw violence
directed against folks
that didn't look like them,
who spoke in foreign tongues,
and believed different things
and wondered
who could do such things.

They prayed when they saw
the dead woman in the alley,
wire hanger by her hand,
and murmured
about the sanctity of life.

They prayed as children
were torn from their mothers' arms
and told one another
that it was a terrible thing
while giving dimes and dollars
to the local orphanage.

They prayed as folks were interned
beneath the desert sun
thankful that the camps
were far from them
and away from public view.

They prayed that hatred

would be banished
and then laughed as lies
and coded words were spoken
to reinforce their fears.

They prayed when folks
were run over.

They prayed when folks
were beaten and brutalized.

They prayed when bombs
were sent through the mail.

They gave their thoughts and prayers
when folks were shot
in the street,
in their place of business,
in their schools,
and in their place of worship
while they prayed.

The Calm Before

A bullet knows no favorites.
It does not distinguish between
friend or foe,
man or woman,
adult or child,
husband or wife,
son or daughter,
cousin or distant friend.

It has no sentiment.
It simply goes where it is aimed
stopping when it is spent
or strikes an object
there along its path of travel.

It does not care
what damage it has done,
which life it has ended
or changed.

It knows nothing of reasons
or the lack thereof,
of rage
or the cold calculation
absent emotion.

It is a tool of destruction,
nothing else,
and whether it is used
for good or ill
is not its concern.

Its flight is swift.
Its life is brief

with ending violent and abrupt,
and once sent it cannot be recalled
much like the fallen
whose end it has been.

There is no remorse
at task well done
only consequence and loss,
tragedy and pain,
and future's brightness dimmed.

We mourn the fallen,
the innocent and the dammed,
and wonder at the reason for it all.

We blame the actor
not the act,
the shooter
not the gun
for release of well-aimed havoc.

We spare no thought for the bullet,
the deliverer of death,
and sorrow,
and oblivion.

For once it has begun its flight,
a bullet knows no favorite.

The Calm Before

Empty seat

There's a place set at the table,
and a glass that's never filled,
where the knife and fork stand ready
for the hand that never will
use them when they're needed
for the vegetables and meat
loved by one who sat there
in the all too empty seat.

They listen for the footsteps
and the slamming of the door
knowing full well all the time
they'll hear them nevermore.
There's a constant expectation
that they'll be there by and by
though the empty chair stands witness
that this is but a lie

to smooth the ragged edges
of the ceaseless grieving mind
that hopes that it's mistaken
and soon will wake to find
that this is but a nightmare,
that this is but a dream
and not the cold hard fact
of an endless primal scream

of rage to fill the heavens,
of anguish held within
for things that will not happen,
for things that should have been
with chances gone forever
due to single, senseless act
that changed the hope filled future

to the ever-present fact

of a place set at the table
with the ever-ready chair
for the one whose voice and laughter
would often fill the air
with stories of adventures,
of pirate ships and kings,
and all the daily sweet delights
that make up childish things.

That place is always empty now
and house is dark and still
with the absence of the one
whose presence somehow filled
their house and hearts with laughter,
that filled their days with joy
with playful times and silly rhymes
of puppy dogs and toys.

But past will never come again
and future now is gone
despite the fact that sun comes up
with each and every dawn.
For they have been left far behind
to wonder at the why
and wander still in endless grief
beneath a leaden sky.

For there's a place set at the table,
and a glass that's never filled,
where the knife and fork stand ready
for the hand that never will
use them when they're needed
for the vegetables and meat
loved by one who sat there
in the all too empty seat.

The Calm Before

Eileen

I go by her house
from time to time.

It's not from nostalgia.
I have no attachment to it.
It just happens to be on the way
to wherever I'm going
or coming back from.

It still strikes me,
even now,
as a sad place,
joyless,
with its shades
of blue clad siding
hiding the pain
that must have lived inside.

They told us,
her classmates,
that she did it there
unloading the barrel
of whatever gun she used
straight into
where it would do
the most good
and leave no chance
for error
or survival.

I cannot imagine
what it was
that led her
to her choice,

what personal horror
or despair
brought her to that end.

She never talked of it,
never seemed more
than just another shy,
reclusive girl
unwilling,
unsure,
or unable
to reach beyond herself
and connect with another
to share whatever pain
she held inside.

I did not know her well.
Perhaps no one truly did
although we saw her every day
in class,
at recess,
and perhaps,
every once in awhile,
at town events.

There are still moments
when I think I see her,
peering out the window
as I drive by.
The face of the thirteen year old,
as she was then,
gazing out at a world
she could never know
trapped as she was
in her own private hell
in a life so oppressive
that she fled it

The Calm Before

with a single act
of desperation.

She merely saw no other escape,
no other chance of relief
from the life she had.

I wonder some days,
as I pass that house of blues,
who and what she would be now
if she had survived,
if the gun had jammed,
or she had simply
changed her mind.

But that didn't happen.
One day she was there.
The next, she was gone,
her private hell ended
and that of others
just begun.

The old man said

The old man said,
"Son, you can't pick the fights you lose
no more than the fights you win.
Shoot, sometimes you might not even know
about the fight you're in.
All you can do is try your best
and when the chips are down,
lose or win, be content
that you have stood your ground.

I think I know a thing or two
just based on where I've been.
Sometimes it seems in the midst of things
that you're nobodies' friend.
But remember as you're standing there,
back against the wall,
don't matter none to anyone
if you rise or fall.

For you sometimes win for losing.
Though that's strange, ain't nothing new.
You'll never lose yourself
if you manage to stay true
to what you know is real
amongst all that other stuff
and I know that telling which is which
is sometimes just darn tough.

But deep inside you know it,
no matter what you say,
whether you've betrayed yourself
or done real good today.
For when it's all been said and done
and you face that final call,

The Calm Before

only you can truly say
if you managed to stand tall."

And as he laid back on his pillow
and drifted slowly off to sleep,
that old man left me with
one final thought to keep.
"It's up to you." He murmured.
Then he smiled soft and sad.
"Do better than the rest of us.
Do better than your Dad."

I think about him often
with tough times all around
and wonder if I'll ever know
what peace he might have found
right there at the finish
of his long, most personal race
when he lay there slowly dying
with sad smile on his face.

For he sometimes won for losing.
Though that's strange, ain't nothing new
'cause he never really lost himself.
He managed to stay true.
And if I'm half the man he was
my troubled mind will rest
and perhaps then I'll find some peace
in hopes I've done my best.

Poison bearing fruit

"You remind me of my daughter."
spoke the ancient man
with a smile broad and kindly.
"You are young as she was
when I saw her last
so many years ago."

Touched despite her hardened years,
the woman smiled in return
and thinking but to ease his burdened mind
replied, "And when was that?"

He started,
as if the words
had touched an open wound,
and he began...

"I saw her last beneath the Jumble trees
upon the plains of Goma,
where jackals played with children
'neath the midday moon.

Such filthy beasts those jackals were
yet they loved the children so
and played with care,
less they muss a curl
upon their golden heads.

They were gentle,
though as savage beasts
they should have torn apart
the partners of their play.
They loved them
and I did hate them for it.

The Calm Before

It was unnatural for the beasts
to love them so.
Yet they did with purest hearts
reveal such love and tender care
that all the children trusted them
instinctively,
my daughter most of all.

For hours she would pet and fawn
upon those ugly brutes
until at dusk,
and only then,
she would come inside,
to stand and stare until the night
had sent them on their way.

Then would she be mine,
though with sad and listless eyes
she would glance at moonless sky.
She would play our games
and talk of days beneath the moon
with jackals at her side,
awaiting sleep
to bring them back again
if but in dreams.

She has been dead to me
these many years
and yet I loathe those jackals still
that had such hold on her
and robbed me of the joy
of her companionship.

For while she was with me
she was with them,
in mind if not in body,
on the plains

with fruit
the common bond between them.

She had a favorite of the beasts,
a large and hideous brute
whose fangs dripped red in setting sun
with drool from stippled tongue
that fell in pools upon the ground
where children laughed
and children played.

It would only play with her,
a constant at her side.
She would tell me of its strength
and how it loved to play
among the grass and winding spots
where roots protrude,
where she and it would lie and rest
beneath the midday moon.

She would speak of this and more
with genuine delight.
It was her one true interest
to speak so when inside.
The beast was there between us
even when I held her fast
and loved her with my heart
and with my life.

She was everything to me
since my wife had died
in the year of falling stones.
But she loved the jackal
and I might not have been alive
so little did she notice
my presence in her life.

The Calm Before

And on the day without a moon,
when jackals slept in hidden lairs,
she would mope and whine and pout
through the day without a playmate,
for the beast was fast asleep
and deaf to her cries
to play their games.

When the beasts awoke at morning
beneath the newborn moon,
the sound of waking calls
would rouse her from her sleep
and send her towards the dawn.

She would race the sun
to see him come
from plains of grass
to this green grove.
And there beneath the trees
they'd share the Jumble fruit,
and eat its juicy, pungent meat,
that ripened when the moon was dark
and jackals slept,
and children cried.

They shared the fruit,
a common meal
that served to seal the bond
between this golden child
and her beast,
until with fruit consumed
they,
with common thought,
began to play.

And with such play my hatred grew.
And in such hatred came a plan.

Grieco

If the beast could be dealt with,
if the jackal was no more,
then daughter of my heart
would in anguish turn to me
and I would share her life
as beast did then.

You say such thoughts betray
a madness deep within.
But I was father to my deepest dreams
and the beast the nightmare of my soul.

The fruit,
the common toy
and meal to seal the bond,
became my instrument of fate,
my weapon to destroy the beast
and gain my daughter's love again.

I gathered one beneath the moon
while still unripe and firm
and saved it for the morning
after moonless day
when beasts returned to play.

I poisoned it.
I filled it full of hatred
clear and pure,
and hid the tainted fruit
within the chest
within my room
for day without a moon
and ripeness
to portend the end of jackal
and beginning of my life again.

The Calm Before

So I waited restlessly
for cycle to begin
and darkened moon
to bring my plan to ripeness.

Time did pass so slowly
and the fruit
did lay within my chest,
a burden and solution sure,
awaiting only day without a moon
to bring it forth
and hatred into play.

I waited
and my anxiousness increased
as each night passed
and moon rose
to grace the morning sky with silvered light
while children laughed
and beasts played.

And in the midst of fevered pulse,
a calming thought would wend its way
to ease my racing heart
and soothe my mind.
Soon,
soon,
it would be done
and chest hid fruit
would end the beast for good.

And then it came,
the day without a moon,
when daughter moped
and whined
and pined for playmate
fast asleep upon the plains of Goma.

And I listened
knowing well that one night more
would end the need for childish cries
and bring her back to me.

In the morn,
before the moon,
I rose and took the fruit
from place within the chest
and placed it in the doorway
where she would stop
and gather ripened fruit for beast to eat.
And with first bite
my plan would be complete
as hatred's poison,
pure and clear,
would end beast's play forever.

In the morning's air
I felt a chill of sweet foreboding
waiting there,
but I proceeded with my plan.

She rose,
my sweetest daughter rose,
a smile on her lips
as cries of jackals filled the sky,
a mournful soulless wail.
It brought her joy,
to me as well
for I knew it soon would end
with me left there to comfort child
for the loss of hated friend.

She saw the fruit and thanked me,
in her customary way,
for putting it there for her to find

The Calm Before

at beginning of the day.
Then with a glad and gleeful heart
she grabbed the fruit and ran
bringing hatred to belovéd beast
and release to me at last.

I saw them softly playing
with the fruit between,
the hatred silent,
waiting
to destroy this happy scene.

When next I looked the day was old
beneath the midday moon.
The deed was done
and hatred eaten
as the fruit had been consumed
and they did lie there peacefully
as others laughed and played
beneath the shady trees
within my private doom.

She has been dead to me,
these many years and more,
a victim of my hate
spilt full between the roots
where she had played.

She had not left her friend
but silent lay
with head on chest
of that gigantic beast
with arm around its furry neck
as they appeared to sleep.

I did go mad they tell me
in rage and spiteful grief

that even in such final rest
the beast my child should keep."

He paused with eyes now focused
on some distant, hidden scene
within his deep set mem'ries
of the long, lost past.
His daughter nodded thoughtfully
and washed his face and hair
and loved him with unspoken words
for who he had once been.

For she had known a loving man,
adored his giving heart,
that shared with her
her child's play
now gone,
long gone,
when hate had led to madness
and dismay.

The fruit had never ripened,
hidden deep within the chest,
so she had picked another Jumble fruit
to share that day with beast.

Tired from the restless night
they were asleep
and nestled in the Jumble root
while others still had played.

No poisoned fruit was eaten.
No hatred was consumed.
She had been lost in mind alone
beneath the midday moon.

With jackal ever present,

The Calm Before

as guardian at her side,
she tended to her father
lest the hatred still inside
should carry him forever
to that scene within his mind
where child and beast still lay
silent on a bed of Goma's grass
and the hatred in the Jumble fruit
had killed the beast at last.

He started as she cared for him
and stared with upturned gaze
to see her face.

Then looking out the window,
at the full, bright silvered moon,
this ancient, brittle man,
with Jumble fruit in hand,
spoke,
"You remind me of my daughter..."

No other

Wars are started
by bad folk
with the worst of intentions.

Power,
that siren
is heeded by many
who would rule
in the name of empire,
in the name of the people,
in the name of God,
or even in their own right.

Wars are started
by good folk
with the best of intents.

Perhaps it is done
in the name of world peace,
or preservation of a way of life
in the face of those
who would change
or destroy it.
Perhaps it is done
simply to sustain an economy
emptied of resources
and of jobs
by depression
or recession
or simply poor choices
made somewhere along the way.

Ideology,
Greed,

The Calm Before

Divine will,
Fear,
all,
all are causes for action
ill or benign
with blood the fuel burned
to make it so
and folk the instruments
used to shape a doom
for one and all
in the course of things.

The end
is seldom as expected
by the ones
who start it all.

Misunderstanding,
miscalculation,
misfortune,
all play their roles
in rendering reasons moot
and causes all the same
across the battlefield.

I fight for God.

I fight for Freedom.

I fight for Country.

I fight for my brothers
who stand with me now
and slowly die
like all the rest
until the final death should come.

Grieco

I fight to stay alive
'til I might leave this place
and live the life of dreams.

I fight for hate,
that none of them
may ever leave this place,
this time,
this site
where death
has more meaning than life
and life
has little or none
for those trapped
until the end should come.

I fight for hope,
that all of this
will not be for naught,
that when it is done
it will have been
worth the price paid
with ground so dearly sowed
with seed that will not grow
save for memories' sake.

I fight because I need to.

I fight because I want to.

I fight because I have no choice
but to be here
where none should be
amidst the carnage and destruction
that mark the ending
and beginning of things.

The Calm Before

Perhaps
there would be fewer wars
if leaders,
good or bad,
fed themselves
to the fury they create
and the causes thus begun
whether won or lost
in the fighting of it.

Perhaps.
But one seldom sees the end
begun by a single act
never mind the endless actions
put in motion
once the first blow is struck,
the first deed done,
and whirlwind unleashed
to sweep away the just and un
along with reasons thought
both right and reasonable.

But regardless of the reasons,
regardless of the right
or wrong of it,
regardless of the outcome,
the war to end all wars
is never so.
There is always another
waiting just beyond our ken,
as aggressors march,
the timid watch,
and peace is undone.

Action
and the lack thereof
may both engender strife

with the proper move,
poorly timed,
turned back against itself
as being rash
or insufficient
for the threat without.

In war
there is no room for doubt,
no place for the hesitant,
no space for delay
or distraction.

For the weak will be conquered,
and the powerful
will bow down
to chains and bondage
unless the will to fight be strong,
the need to resist urgent,
and the force of arms
equal to the task.

Tyrants need only use
the illusion,
the dream of peace
to achieve their ends
knowing that those
who might act against them
will be frozen by their dream,
nay their need
for peace
to be more than illusion,
more than simple transition
between one war and the next.

And as the peaceful
wait in fevered hope

The Calm Before

that it will not,
cannot come here,
armies march,
reason fails,
and states are overthrown.

In the end,
there is no other choice.
Conquer or be conquered.
Fight or be a slave.
Stand by and watch
in hope that reason
and the right will prevail
or join and fight
so that your children
and then theirs
will know the peace
of which you dream
and the world
that still might be
once armies march,
sacrifice is made,
and reason and intent
forgot.

As I watched you go

I watched you go
and did not know
that I would never see you here
caressed by summer's breeze.

I watched you go
and did not know
that I would have mere words
to hold
against the sudden chill of autumn.

I watched you go
and did not know
that winter's snow
would find me still
in deepest black,
a contrast to the silent hills
still waiting your return.

I watched you go
and did not know
that spring would please me not
without your voice and warmth
to make it real
and welcome to my sight.

I watched you go
and did not know
that this would be
the last vision of happiness,
that Death's cruel hand
would encircle yours
and draw you thence
beyond my world

The Calm Before

with singleness of purpose
and no regard for summer's breeze,
autumn's chill,
winter's silent hills,
and springtime's meaning
to the world
and me.

I watched you go
and did not know
that I would miss you so
with no recourse for the aching heart
that mourns your absence
with every pulse of life within.

It is but an instant
and yet it seems forever
since our last embrace.
Too brief,
too brief by far
against this endless waste
of waiting for the next
with sure knowledge
that it cannot be.

And so,
though rain bring
swift assurance of renewal
and new life,
I sit alone.

And though sweet spring
should bring its warmth
and joy to all the world,
still I mourn.

For what was precious

is now gone.

What was real and sure and right
is no more.

Though spirit live
and life remain
it cannot comfort this flesh.
It cannot warm this cheek.
It cannot hold this hand
that needs yours so.

Love remains
though you are absent.

Spring returns
but brings no joy
for all I did not know
as I watched you
go.

The Calm Before

That tattered, battered cloth

It bore a bit of color
that tattered, battered cloth
and they had sworn beneath it
to win at any cost,
to stand while there was daylight,
to last throughout the night,
and so it waved above them
as witness to the fight.

They didn't shrink or waver
but answered to the call.
Each knew with dreadful certainty
that many there would fall.
And when the cannons challenged,
they answered with their own.
With iron balls as seeds did they
the field of death thus sow.

And so it waved,
and so it waved
as they lay behind the hill
waiting for their moment
in the early morning chill

"Rise up. Rise up me boyos!"
came the call from Sergeant John
and so as one they rose to arms
from the shelter they had found.
And still the cannons thundered
and still the iron flew
as they steeled themselves for battle
and the carnage to ensue.

Grieco

"Be mindful now they're comin.'"
came the call from down the line
as the sun shone down upon them
with the weather clear and fine.
They could clearly see them
through the smoke, a field of gray
and each man marked his target
for their first shot of the day.

And yet it waved,
and yet it waved
as their volley then rang out
and from amidst the mayhem
they heard their Sergeant shout

"Give 'em lead for breakfast
and send them straight to Hell!
We'll see 'em all dead at the last
while your children all will tell
the story of your glory,
the story of this day,
when you stood before these mothers
in the fury of the fray.

Yeah give 'em lead for breakfast
and give 'em shot for lunch
and follow that with grape
for their bellies if they bunch.
And if they close by supper
we'll still stand strong and brave
with blades, swords, and bayonets
we'll send them to their graves."

And still it waved,
and still it waved
above the bloody ground
as the guns roared their thunder

The Calm Before

spewing death amidst the sound.

And still the cannons thundered
as the men all stood their ground
though many a brave soul
a resting place there found
while the screams of those still living
mixed with silence of the dead
and many did swear later
that the ground itself bled red.

And when the gray cloud parted,
the foe was close at last
though round ball filled their bellies
and lead shot broke their fast.
And when they crashed together
the lines blurred blue and gray
in hand-to-hand they'd settle
this portion of the day.

And still it waved,
and still it waved
defended at all cost
with battle in the balance
unknown who'd won or lost.

And then they broke, some running
across the battlefield
while others on their knees
to bayonets did yield
the hopes of all their futures,
the memories of their pasts.
They never gave up fighting
even as they breathed their last.

"Reform, reform me boyos
with the rifle and the gun.

Shoot those sorry bastards.
Kill 'em while they run.
Then take a drink of water,
pass ammo down the line.
I'm proud of you me boyos.
You did just fine, just fine."

And still it waved,
and still it waved
above their weakened ranks
where each man paused in wonder
and gave his silent thanks.

"Now bind up all the wounded
and gather up the dead.
Be grateful that you're gatherin'
and not there in their stead.
But be watchful while you're doin'
and cry out at any sign
if those bleedin' bloody bastards
try to come agin the line."

They came twice more that morning,
though fewer came each time,
but none came even close
to carrying the line.
They came again at midday
and then in afternoon
and when they stopped at evening
it couldn't be too soon.

For though it waved,
for though it waved
as symbol of their might
if they came again that day
t'would be their final fight.

The Calm Before

"Lie down, lie down me boyos
and enjoy a bit o' rest.
If they come tomorrow
I'll want you at your best."
More slept than merely slumbered
beneath the autumn moon
with only scouts and pickets
lonely pondering their doom.

They lay there until morning
when the day broke cold and clear.
The scouts found that the enemy
that night had disappeared.
They'd slipped past all the pickets
retreating to the rear
abandoning the field
where they'd found the cost so dear.

And so it waved,
and so it waved
by mounds of blue and gray
but no one knew the difference
in the breaking of the day.

They lay there where they'd fallen
in the morning cold and frost
and those who'd merely slumbered
could measure what they'd lost.
They searched to find the wounded
there lying with the dead
and paused by fallen comrades
to take their daily bread.

And when the task was finished,
they'd done all they could do.
They gathered 'neath the banner
though their numbers now were few.

Grieco

They gathered round the banner.
Some comfort there they sought.
It bore a bit of color
that tattered, battered cloth.

The Calm Before

Glory

Glory.
They say there's glory in this
but I see none of it.
There's only the dead and the dying
and those fortunate enough
to postpone that fate awhile longer.

There's no sense to it,
who dies and who doesn't.
It isn't skill as much as luck sometimes
but even the lucky ones die
when strength falters
and skill won't fill the gap
'til fortune does.

The statesmen say that war
is a necessary evil,
but they do not fight it.

Some use war
to spread their faith,
only too willing to sacrifice others
for the glory of God
and their own power.

Some use war
as a means to an end,
an instrument of power
to remove a policy impediment
or an ideological foe.
Yet somehow their hands stay clean.

Some use war
as a last chance grasp for survival

against a foe bent on dominion
determined to destroy all who disagree
or who stand for other creeds.
They serve until an end is reached.

All are different,
yet all are the same
depending on where you stand,
which threat you see,
what choices you pursue.

And with all of these come Glory.

Glory.
Destroyed lives,
vanished dreams,
the end of hopes,
snatched away by the realities of war.

Glory.
Shattered land,
desolation where beauty once shone,
men and women maimed and crippled,
debris scattered as the cost of policies
enacted for the common good.

Glory.
Those that fight
know the bright of day
and dark of night,
the joy of survival
and the sorrow
when those held close
do not.

Glory.
When it all comes down

The Calm Before

to thrust and stab,
duck and run,
sound and fury,
live or die on the turn of chance,
the misplaced foot
or an errant shell.

Glory.
We teach ourselves
with endless stories of sacrifice,
of honor,
of charges made,
objectives seized,
and last stands
that made the future possible,
that Glory is real,
that it can be gained
if we are but willing
to give ourselves for the common good,
if we be guided by our leaders,
our faith,
and the statesmen
with their lofty goals
and private ambitions.

Ask the dead.

Ask the dying.

The need may have been great,
the struggle worth the cost
in lives and dreams and liberties lost.
But Glory is for the living,
for those who must be convinced
that this is worthwhile,
that this must be borne
again and again

as duty calls,
armies march,
and death and necessity prevail.

Others may call this Glory
but I see none of it.

The Calm Before

Still life

They were boys and young
when they left
the sun warm upon their cheeks
as they walked away.

They did not look back
so focused were they
on the way ahead
with life's vibrant richness
full upon them.

I have a picture of them
here
as they were then
eyes bright with visions of adventure,
their faces lit by smiles
that spoke of happy anticipation
of the journey yet to come.

It is all I have of them,
this picture,
to remember them by,
frozen in time
at the moment of their leaving.

They were perfect in their youth,
eager for adventure,
with no thought
of what they left behind.

It is ever so
that those who stay
to watch them go
are soon forgot

within the rush to see,
to know
what lies ahead
just around the corner
of a life not lived
in the straight and narrow confines
of a safe,
local place.

Despite the letters we received,
I doubt if they lingered long
wondering how we fared back home
while they in frenzied haste
lived,
as though there were no tomorrow,
reveling in sense and sounds,
experiencing each in turn
until there were no more to have.

They trained them well
and turned them into men
and soldiers
ready for the fight
and enemy to come.
And when the fighting came at last,
they acquitted themselves
as men within the fray,
ever bold in the face
of foe and horrors
those who did return
would never speak of.

They survived until the end
and it is one of life's bitter ironies
that it be so,
that one stray round,
with but one day yet to go,

The Calm Before

should have found them
huddled deep within their bunker
waiting for the peace to come.

I'd like to think they were laughing,
sharing some private joke
as they were wont to do,
just before the shell fell.
But I suppose
I will never know for sure.
Still…

They never knew.
Never felt the impact
or the blast
that followed quick upon it
with death
swift and sure
as the silence that followed behind.

I have heard it said
that it was a blessing
that it came so fast,
with no warning,
fear,
or suffering.

I have heard it said
that it was a tragedy
that they should perish then
with the end in view.

All I know
is that I miss them,
bright faced and smiling
as the sun shone,
the wind blew,

and camera captured
the memory of them
as they were.

They were boys and young
when they left…

The Calm Before

Gold Star

We are proud of our children.
We are proud that they chose
to serve their country.

We respect their choice,
their decision to pursue
a life of hardship and deprivation,
a life that led them far from home,
that separated them from family
and friends,
a life of sacrifice
that ultimately brought them
here,
to us,
one final time.

It is not for us to question their sacrifice
or the choices that brought them,
in this manner,
home.

We may regret the need,
we may decry the policies,
we may rail at the circumstances
of their deaths,
but we honor them,
and we will never forget
the people they were
before.

In the end we receive a star
to mark all they were
and what they sought to accomplish
through their choices,

their sacrifice,
their service to this country,
and we accept this star in humility,
sadness,
bitterness,
and grief.

Humility,
that our children came to view
the common good
as greater than their own.

Sadness.
that they will never see
the common good,
the future they have created
through their sacrifice.

Bitterness,
that it had to be our children
who sacrificed their futures
for those who remain complacent
in their comforts
and everyday concerns.

Grief,
at the loss of those we loved
and raised
and guided
to be the people we honor
for their choices,
for their sense of duty,
for their dedication
to a vision of a world
others could not see.

This star is a remembrance

The Calm Before

of those forever gone,
a symbol for those left behind
of courage,
of a devotion to duty,
long thought gone,
vanished in a world
of selfishness and greed.

It honors those valiant few,
those courageous folk
who believed that the future
was more important than their lives,
that their hopes for a peaceful world
were greater than their personal dreams,
that peace for all
was a greater good
than their own personal safety.

We shall miss them.
We do now.
And it is hollow comfort
to have this star
instead of our children,
to hold this fabric
instead of those we love,
to hear your condolences
instead of their laughter,
their wisdom,
and their voices
to explain the need,
to explain the reasons,
to provide the comfort
we so sorely need
to accept their absence,
to accept their sacrifice,
to accept
this Gold Star.

Onward to Thermopylae

Hooray!
The clash of arms is silent now
and settled to the earth
as carrion crows
begin their grisly work
to rid the site of folly's end
and ambition's sure sowing
of the soil with those that were men.

Hooray!
The air has cleared of smoke
and clear blue skies
are full above this scene
of earnest celebration
for the ending
and beginning of the world.

For end has come to those
who lie in tortured repose
while those who move
can only wonder
at the splendor of a day
seen with unshrouded eyes
and hope restored.

Hooray!
For from this day
will glorious future come
with teachers pointing to their wards,
"Look, here upon this spot
did valiant soldiers strive and die
to bring forth the peace
that we know now."
and,

The Calm Before

"Here was born our nationhood."
and,
"These precious few
that gave so much
that we might live
to stand here and remember."
Hooray!

But in the falling dust
there are no victors,
for the foes
are much alike
in their silent view
of what they both have wrought.

Statues to the future do they lie.
Martyrs of the present are they now.
Children of the past
whose days were stolen
and used as payment
in uncertain times
for certain cause
and then spilt upon the ground
as promise for a kinder tomorrow.

Hooray!
They sleep now.
A phrase to cover death
and render it impotent,
protecting us
from its destructive realness
and decay
that we may live in this,
our time,
and speak well
of those who died before,
in unsought shedding of the spirit.

Grieco

For they were fools
and wise men both
but now are joined
where all have found
the common thread
of this,
our fabric.

What bitter dregs of memories
lie upon this field?
What hopes and dreams lost
that shall not be found again?
Heroes and cowards all,
they await
for future's benediction.

Hooray.
The clash of arms is silent now.
But it is ever so
when future lies between two points
and waits for our decision
for the course to go.

And so,
this moment's past
becomes our guide
in so choosing present's course
with these,
and all before,
our silent partners
in the struggle yet ahead.
They have earned our respect.
It is we who must now earn theirs.

Each dream vanished
in the endless depths of time
we must replace with one of ours.

The Calm Before

For each hope destroyed by ending here
we must find our way to its restoration.

In each death upon this field
we must find meaning,
and make sense from senselessness,
and reason in our present lives.

Hooray.
The clash of arms is silent now,
But never long, never, long,
and it is we who now
must face the test
in this our day,
to gird ourselves
to face what comes.
May the gods be merciful
if we should fail,
as these did not.

Hooray.
And if the grass should grow untended here
with reason and the causes long forgot
then we shall be the less for it.
And if we should forget these brave few,
whose days are dust beneath our feet,
then we shall have forgot ourselves.

For we are they in different clothes
with hopes and dreams the same.
And could we shout, "Arise!",
we would recognize
our fathers and our sons,
our daughters and our mothers,
dearest loves
and most appalling foes,

united in the unknown land of yesterday
beyond our touch or ability to know.

Hooray.
The clash of arms is silent now.

Look.
Lest we forget
and hot and bitter wind
descend to reap this generation
of its finest and most cherished dreams.

Remember.
That some things are worth the price
of this most tragic scene.

Weep.
That any should come to this end,
this place,
of ultimate sacrifice and sorrow.

Dream.
Of better worlds,
where war is but a distant thought
to those who study past times.

Hope.
That we shall never meet
upon a field like this
in circumstances dire and clear
with future's consequence.

Hooray.
The clash of arms is silent now.
Hooray.

The Calm Before

Impressions of a Winter's Day

The drum beat slowly,
a counterpoint
to dreams no longer dreamt,
hopes no longer held,
thoughts no longer shared
with those gathered near.

The winter wind
cut through coats and capes alike
leaving only chilled memories
of a greater warmth
and cold comfort
to those in search of more.

Quiet murmurs 'neath the wind,
hidden under crackle of unfurled flags,
met muted creaking from the harnessed team
drawing caisson down the lane.

Silent,
save for wind
and flags
and harnessed team,
all moved along the cobbled path
to destination,
stark and lonely 'neath the graying sky.

Spoken words then,
alone against the wind,
caught and flung
so that one must strain to hear them
pass and disappear
there among the stones.

"No greater love…"
"… last ounce of devotion…"
"… service to God and country…"
"… that all might live…"
"… freedom, peace,…"
"… just and lasting rest…"
"… embraced by God…"
"… remembered for this sacrifice…"
"… forever and ever…"

And with the last "Amen"
the music comes,
unwanted sound that signifies
too much,
too soon,
too final
as the last notes are torn
and vanish in the wind
followed by volley,
honor that it is,
that marks the end
save for folded cloth
gently pressed in waiting hands.

Subdued,
those gathered leave
in clumps of twos and threes
until but one remains
with last flower clenched
and then let go
as though a breath
too long held
was finally released.

Then,
bereft of flower
and of more,

The Calm Before

that one turns and walks away.

A bird cries once
and then is still
leaving only box,
and earth,
and sky,
and wind.

Among the Stones

I stood among the stones today
with memories from the past
etched with chisel's sharpened blade
to mark the spot
where we have laid
these remnants of ourselves.

They rest
but do not sleep,
within this confine of dirt and dust
away from eyes that see only ending
and threat to their existence.

No one would choose to visit this lonely place
on such a gray and wind-swept day
with chill to touch these living bones
and give them sense of those
that lay beneath in semblance of repose.

Why I came I cannot say
for there is naught but stone
to speak for those who speechless lie
awaiting future's benediction
or benign neglect.

They fade
to be but footnotes on a page of history
in tome upon some musty shelf
visited only by scholars
searching to explain
what brought these fellows here
with only me as guest
to reason with the wind.

The Calm Before

I stand among these stones
listening for the voices of the dead
to guide the footsteps of the living.
But their silent voices
are only echoes in the wind
carried far beyond these chiseled stones
to where I cannot hear them.

I cannot,
should not stay
for reason does defy
the urge that brought me here
to stand
and contemplate the wind
across this empty place.

Life bids me return
to a brighter, warmer place.
But I do feel for those so left behind
and gone from where they could have answered
had the questions been spoken
and the wind more kind.

And if we truly follow
on the path where they have gone,
with simple words in chiseled stone
to mark the passage of our days,
then we shall know the unknowable,
and have the wind-swept truth
in answer to questions strewn
upon this barren ground
as I stood among the stones today.

Alone

We are a solitary people
living solitary lives.

We are born alone.

We live within these shells,
alone.

We pass from them to what awaits,
alone.

There is no changing this.
But there is hope.

Hope
that we may touch another's life
and be touched in return,
that we may ease the quiet loneliness
which all share,
with which we greet the dawn
and meet the night.

Hope
that we might make a difference
in between,
that we might love,
and in loving
create a world of possibilities
not otherwise conceivable.

It is this hope that gives life meaning.
It is this hope that keeps us sane
when all would seem but madness
and the chance of a random world.

The Calm Before

It is this hope that gives us strength
to persist and bless the daylight
for the chances found therein.

It would be best to make the most of these
and live with no thought of what comes after.
We cannot change it.
It is a circumstance of fate,
of life,
that it is so.

And when the night does come,
it will not matter if we have won or lost,
laughed or cried,
walked or run
across our span of time.

It will be as a dream,
dreamt in the living of it
with memories scant refuge
for the fading mind
as vision dims,
breath comes hard,
and darkness beckons.

But even then
as light fades
and chances become few,
and then none,
there is still hope.

We live,
laugh,
and love.
We hope
that we are more
than the sum of our days

so that we may be comforted
and not regret our follies
and our chosen paths.

We cannot know
if what we do will last
or fade with the light
to be lost with the dream,
to vanish with the memories
and end with us.

And faced with that end,
we hope
that we have been wrong.

Hope
that there is more yet to be.

Hope
that the darkness is not an end
but a beginning unimagined in its possibilities.

Hope
that in those final, solitary moments
we will find that we are more than ourselves,
more than our choices,
more than the sum of our days,
and that we are not
after all,
alone.

The Calm Before

Stories

We tell ourselves the stories of our past
and laugh at how naïve we were,
wonder at the youth thus spent,
marvel at the distance traveled,
and embrace our common destiny,
here,
now,
as we grasp for what was
and may still be
within our hearts.

It is not far.
It is as close as yesterday
though today that distance
seems beyond our reach.

Were we ever so?
Were our hearts ever so pure,
our thoughts ever so firmly set
upon the right of things
without regard to consequence?

Were we ever so disdainful
of fate,
of destiny,
and a future
beyond what we could see,
within our minds at least?

And when that future came to be,
with all the twists and turns
unforeseen in their occurrence,
did we rail against it?
Did we scream our outrage at the sky

that this was not, after all,
what we had envisioned in our dreams
when we dreamt them
all so many years ago?

Or did we shrug,
as acceptance replaced defiance,
as necessity replaced dreams,
and we sat before the fading fire of ambition
and told ourselves
that this was what we wanted all along?

It is how we live, these stories.
It is how we make peace with ourselves
for what we did not become
and what we did not do
with all the dreams we held so dear
in our youth.

And if the stories change with the telling
and glory missed becomes the source of pride,
what of it?

What harm that we be more than what we were
since there is no one to know the difference
now?

We tell ourselves the stories of our past
and laugh at how it all turned out,
laugh at what we thought we knew.

The Calm Before

Gatekeeper

I have been to the mountain.
I have held the secret of existence
on the palm of my hand
and wondered at its simplicity.

I have watched the first stray light
pierce the shadowed vaults of night
to bring forth the newborn day.

I have watched the winged wonders of the air
and smelt the freshly scented fragrance
of a thousand flowering trees.
And I miss the mountain.

I have walked the midnight paths,
leaving stars like dust
behind me as I passed.
I have raised the Tempest,
bending worlds beneath my will.

I have passed through phantomed depths of ocean
to move untouched upon the shore of chance.
Still, I miss the mountain.

Past and Future are the same
with Present fire enough to warm the soul
of one who has traveled far.
What glory in being.
What freedom in unshackled existence.
Such wonders did I know
before I came to be.

Rage not,
for the time for rage is past

though certain memories stay unbidden
upon the scars of possibility.

Upon the mountain was I one of many
dwelling in the essence of that place.
Here,
I am one of few who guard the entrance.

By my choice, I am here among you.
Yet do I yearn,
for a moment's peace within,
upon the mountain,
does equal ten without
upon stages built of life's imaginings
and the dance that marks them so.

So many stages,
with every dance
twisting at the fabric of existence
'til its true color be revealed.

And once revealed,
that stage is struck
with yet another
waiting in its time
to take its place
with dance then born anew.

And though dancers be pale echoes
of what they might yet be,
even they shall know
the beauty of the mountain
while I must stay
'til last steps are complete.

Dance on across my dreams.
Climb onward to the heights.

The Calm Before

Breathe the raptured air
and fly among the winds
that share the very nature of being.

I remain below,
a guardian of my chosen fate,
to be the essence of my chosen state.
And I miss the mountain.

Half faced man

Half faced man
gazing down
upon this place,
what are your thoughts
this day?

Do you see the boundaries
of the earth and seas
or think them imagined things
changed by time and movement
and never really there at all?

Do you envy the bounty
of your sister's gifts
enjoyed by the favored few,
fortunate in birth
and lucky in location,
or are such things
beneath the notice
of your barren gaze?

Jealous moon,
do you resent the sun
for its glory?

Do you circle round your sister
and think,
why not me?

Do you pause,
reflection of a greater glory,
to ponder your captive fate?

The Calm Before

Silent do you rest
and hide your thoughts from me
but had you heart
I would hear it break
with the injustice of it
that you should
in sad reflection stay
beyond the reach
of sister's joy.

Shhh.
Tell me naught of truth
or lies
or other matters
seen with your eyes.
I wish to know them not
for I have changed my mind
on this.

Oh half faced man,
tell me not your secrets
for I could not bear
the sorrow of your tale
forever in the night
with nothing but reflected light
to take you on your way.

Grieco

A small thing,
almost imperceptible,
and unnoticed
in the greater scheme of things,
and yet
it changes everything
once the word is spoken,
the path taken,
and the deed done.

ABOUT THE AUTHOR

Born and raised in a small rural town, the author left to pursue higher education and a career which took him to different parts of the world. After a lifetime listening to the whisper of the wind, the burble of a brook, and the sound of songbirds all imparting their wisdom, he's returned to his roots, spending his days as a country gentleman, taking the time now and then to put some words on paper.

Find more from Pat at pat-grieco.com

www.ingramcontent.com/pod-product-compliance
Lightning Source LLC
Chambersburg PA
CBHW032142040426
42449CB00005B/357